Reading Together

THIS IS THE
BEAR

Read it together

This Is the Bear is a gentle story of the rivalry between the two most important friends in a boy's life: his dog and his teddy. Many children will be able to relate this story to their own experiences with friends or siblings.

> *This is the bear who fell in the bin. This is the dog who pushed him in.*

> **Naughty dog!**

Talking together about the book helps children to understand the meanings of the story and the way it is written.

> *Stop, stop!* shouts the boy, but I don't think they can hear him, do you?

> **No, they're driving away.**

With the strong patterns of rhythm and rhyme, children learn how to predict the next word. Rhyme also helps them to see that some words sound and look alike.

This is the bear who went to the dump and fell on the pile ...

with a bit of a bump.

You can encourage children to use the pictures to work out what the words say and predict what will happen next.

He didn't really think he was lost – he could see them coming!

When children enjoy one story it can prompt them to make up another about their own lives or one that mixes together other stories they know well.

When my teddy was lost I didn't think he'd come back.

But Kay found him at the playgroup, didn't she?

We hope you enjoy reading this book together.

For Barbara, who makes bears
S.H.

For Edward (Teddy) Craig
H.C.

First published 1986 by Walker Books Ltd
87 Vauxhall Walk, London SE11 5HJ

This edition published 2005

2 4 6 8 10 9 7 5 3

Text © 1986 Sarah Hayes
Illustrations © 1986 Helen Craig
Introductory and concluding notes © 1998 CLPE/LB Southwark

Printed in China

ISBN 1-4063-0057-8

www.walkerbooks.co.uk

THIS IS THE
BEAR

Written by
Sarah Hayes

Illustrated by
Helen Craig

WALKER BOOKS
AND SUBSIDIARIES

LONDON · BOSTON · SYDNEY · AUCKLAND

This is the bear
who fell in the bin.

This is the dog
who pushed him in.

This is the man
who picked up the sack.

This is the driver
who would not come back.

This is the bear
who went to the dump

and fell on the pile
with a bit of a bump.

This is the boy
who took the bus

and went to the dump
to make a fuss.

This is the man
in an awful grump
who searched

and searched
and searched the dump.

This is the bear
all cold and cross

who did not think
he was really lost.

This is the dog
who smelled the smell

of a bone

and a tin

and a bear as well.

This is the man
who drove them home –

the boy, the bear
and the dog with a bone.

This is the bear
all lovely and clean

who did not say
just where he had been.

This is the boy
who knew quite well,

but promised his friend
he would not tell.

And this is the boy
who woke up in the night
and asked the bear
if he felt all right –
and was very surprised
when the bear shouted out,
"How soon can we have
another day out?"

Read it again

Telling tales

The dog has his own tale to tell about the lost bear.
Use the pictures to tell the dog's story.

Speech balloons

The speech balloons add another way of telling the story. Read through the book using the speech balloons to act out the events of the story.

The bear hunt

You could play "bear hunt" games with a favourite teddy, taking it in turns to find the bear.

The next adventure

The story ends with the promise of another adventure. What else might happen to the bear? With your help, children can make up another bear adventure or share stories about their own bears.

Other rhymes

This Is the Bear has a similar pattern to *This Is the House That Jack Built*, another rhyme that's good to read aloud. There are three other *This Is the Bear* stories you might enjoy: *This Is the Bear and the Scary Night*, *This Is the Bear and the Picnic Lunch* and *This Is the Bear and the Bad Little Girl*. All these are available from libraries and bookshops.